Trivia Madness

1000 Fun Trivia Questions About Anything

Trivia Quiz Questions and Answers Vol 2

By
Bill O'Neill

ISBN-13:978-1532745201

DISCLAIMER

This book contain trivia questions and answers and funny facts that will make any quiz challenge enjoyable. I hope you like movie trivia and music trivia because this book has it, a thousand of them! Enjoy the quizzes!

What company introduced the Stratocaster style of electric guitar in 1954?

Fender

, ·

In the 1896 Olympic Games, what awards were won?

First place winners got a silver medal and an olive branch. Second place got a bronze. Third place got nothing.

, ·

What country has a larger surface area than Pluto?

Russia

, ·

What university is older than the Aztec Empire?

Oxford University

, ·

Which country still executed people by guillotine when Star Wars: A New Hope was released in 1977?

France

What electronics company began by selling trading cards?

Nintendo

, .

What minerals are forged on Jupiter and Saturn?

Diamonds

, .

The oldest written record of the name 'Jessica' is found as the name of a character in what Shakespeare play?

The Merchant of Venice

, .

What does the nursery rhyme Humpty Dumpty suggest Humpty Dumpty is?

An egg (Nowhere in the nursery rhyme does it say that Humpty Dumpty is an egg)

, .

What is the national animal of Scotland?

Unicorn

There is enough water in what lake to cover all of North and South America in one foot of liquid?

Lake Superior

, .

What American city is further south than Rome?

New York City

, .

What is the closest US state to Africa?

Maine

, .

What is the most common name in world?

Muhammad

, .

What is the most commonly used team nickname in American sports?

Eagles

, .

In playing cards what is the only one of the kings without a mustache?

King of Hearts

What is missing on the face of Leonardo da Vinci's painting 'Mona Lisa'?

Mona Lisa has no clearly visible eyebrows

, ·

The poem "Defence of Fort McHenry" later became the lyrics to what song?

The Star-Spangled Banner

, ·

What cannot fly if their body temperature is less than 86 degrees?

Butterflies

, ·

What are the only mobile National Monuments in the United States?

San Francisco Cable cars

, ·

What animals have the longest pregnancy in the animal kingdom at 22 months?

Elephants

What species produces 100 million young in her lifetime?

Female oyster

, •

What part of the human body is composed of 75 percent water?

Brain

, •

What dog breed can follow a scent that is four days old?

Bloodhounds

, •

Who can see up to sixteen sunrises and sunsets every day?

Astronauts orbiting Earth

, •

What country has more sheep than people?

New Zealand

, •

What was the first food eaten in space by an American astronaut?

Applesauce

The wind on what planet blows
up to 1,243 miles an hour?

Neptune

, •

What insect has more muscles than a human?

Caterpillar

, •

The first email was sent in what year?

1971

, •

What condiment was originally sold
as a digestive extract?

Ketchup

, •

Before the invention of toothpaste, what did
people use to clean their teeth?

Charcoal

, •

What is the hottest planet of our solar system?

Venus

How many moons does the planet Jupiter have?

Jupiter has 63 moons

, •

What were the first passengers on a hot-air balloon?

A sheep, a duck, and a rooster

, •

What creature has 3,000 teeth and 4 noses?

Slugs

, •

What type of metal can be made into soap?

Stainless steel

, •

What country opened the first elderly retirement home for dogs?

Japan

, •

The insults aimed at what politician later became the symbol for the Democratic Party?

Andrew Jackson (Jackass)

What German leader once issued a manifesto which stated his people must drink beer, and not coffee?

Frederick the Great

, •

What city in Italy does not get direct sunlight for 83 days a year due to the surrounding mountains?

Viganella

, •

75 % of all tornadoes occur in what country?

United States

, •

In the 19th Century, what animal, previously only seen in the forest, was released into American parks for entertainment?

Squirrels

, •

What word was introduced in a 1920 science fiction play by the Czech writer Karel Capek?

Robot

Whenever a person's true identity is unknown, what name is used on legal documents?

John or Jane Doe

, .

What is the national game of Afghanistan?

Buzkashi (goat-grabbing)

, .

What mammal lives on every continent except Antarctica?

Bats

, .

What was the first country to use flamethrowers in World War I?

Germany

, .

Approximately how many pictures are uploaded to Facebook each month?

More than 2.5 billion

, .

Who is regarded as the father of American football?

Walter Camp

What unique degree is offered at the University of Indiana?

Bowling Management

, .

Condoms during the Renaissance were made out of what material?

Animal intestines

, .

From which country did French horns originate?

Germany

, .

Arabic numerals originated in which country?

India

, .

Catgut, a material for the strings of musical instruments, is made from what?

Sheep or goat intestines

, .

What type of creature is a Bombay duck made of?

Fish (specifically a Bummalo fish)

In the French medieval version of "Cinderella", what were Cinderella's slippers made from?

Squirrel fur

, •

In what continent did camels first evolve?

North America

, •

Where was Canadian Club whiskey first distilled?

Detroit, Michigan USA

, •

In what country was the game Chinese Checkers invented?

Germany

, •

In what month is the Munich Oktoberfest beer festival held?

September

, •

When is Red October recognized in Russia?

November

The Portuguese Man-of-War (a sea-dwelling jellyfish-like invertebrate) alludes to a warship design devised in which country?

England

, •

What are sticks of blackboard chalk made from?

Gypsum(Calcium Sulphate)

, •

What are toy marbles made from?

Glass

, •

What color are white grapes?

Green

, •

What color is a (male) purple finch?

Red(most females are brown)

, •

What color is orange blossom?

White

What color is the black box (flight recorder) on a plane?

Orange

, •

In what country did baseball originate?

England

, •

What creatures are the Canary Islands named after?

Dogs

, •

What is kitchen tin foil made from?

Aluminum

, •

In the children's book, where is Paddington Bear from?

Peru

, •

Which insect shorted out an early supercomputer and inspired the term "computer bug"?

Moth

Now used to refer to a cat, the word "tabby" is derived from the name of a district of what capital?

Baghdad

, •

Who did artist Grant Wood use as the model for the farmer in his classic painting "American Gothic"?

His dentist

, •

Moses received what list on Mt. Sinai?

Ten Commandments

, •

What gunfighter wound up a New York City sports reporter?

Bat Masterson

, •

What herb's name comes from belief that it will lengthen life and increase wisdom?

Sage

In golf, what is 2 under par for a hole?

Eagle

, .

If the body were a car, what would be the carburetors?

Lungs

, .

Building what up with steroids has caused sports controversy?

Muscles

, .

Babies have more than 300, while adults have only 206 of what?

Bones

, .

What is a group of senators who vote together for a specific purpose?

Bloc

, .

What is a French phrase for food items, ordered separately?

A la carte

What do the British call “the lift”?

Elevator

, •

What state boasts Mount Rushmore?

South Dakota

, •

What tropical fruit is a traditional garnish for ham?

Pineapple

, •

What is the state flower of Kansas?

Sunflower

, •

Unless he dies or resigns, the only way to remove a president from office is by what process?

Impeachment

, •

The geometrical ratio 3.14159265 or Pi is symbolized by what letter in the Greek alphabet?

Sixteenth

What month's birthstone is turquoise, and its flower, the holly?

December

, ·

Among the symbols in what are the sun, a hanged man and a fool?

Tarot cards

, ·

The Battle of Bunker Hill occurred on what hill?

Breed's Hill

, ·

In the Bible, who were the three sons of Adam?

Seth, Abel & Cain

, ·

Who was reelected vice president of the U.S. In 1996?

Al Gore

In Monopoly, what square will set you back $200 or 10% of your total score?

Income Tax

' ·

Who played Mr. Freeze in the movie "Batman and Robin"?

Arnold Schwarzenegger

' ·

What material can be shaped by hand & fired in a kiln to make pottery?

Clay

' ·

What plant-eater named for the 3 horns on its face was at least 25 feet long?

Triceratops

' ·

What astronaut said, "Houston... the Eagle has landed"?

Neil Armstrong

What cracker was introduced by Nabisco in 1934 and named to conjure up an image of wealth & glamour?

Ritz

, •

An outbreak of disease is known as what?

Epidemic

, •

Who launched her "Everyday" collection at Kmart in 1997?

Martha Stewart

, •

What duke of Bohemia is remembered in a Christmas carol as a "good king"?

Wenceslas

, •

What female name is attributed to the 1904 play "Peter Pan"?

Wendy

, •

What is the fashion doll Barbie's full name?

Barbara Millicent Roberts

What is the dot over the lower case "i" called?

Tittle

, •

If dropped in a glass of fresh champagne, what will bounce up and down continuously from the bottom of the glass to the top?

A raisin

, •

What animal can die if it goes into heat and cannot find a mate?

A female ferret

, •

What are the real dimensions of a 2 X 4 board?

1 1/2 by 3 1/2 inches

, •

Because metal was scarce, the Oscars given out during World War II were made of what material?

Plaster

What actor was once Howard Hughes's bodyguard?

Wilford Brimley

, •

In a 2008 survey, 58% of British teens thought who was a real guy?

Sherlock Holmes

, •

What was President Taft's answer to Roosevelt's Teddy Bear?

Billy Possum

, •

What was invented during WWII, when an Italian pastry maker mixed hazelnuts into chocolate to extend his chocolate ration?

Nutella

, •

What animal says hello with kisses?

Prairie dogs

In the mid-1980s, who was the voice of Charlie Brown's sister Sally?

Fergie (Black Eyed Peas)

, •

What national symbol was designed by a 17 year old high school student?

50-star American Flag

, •

What football coach played Screech's cousin on a 1996 episode of "Saved by the Bell: The New Class"?

Jim Harbaugh

, •

Who wrote Barry Manilow's hit song titled "I Write the Songs"?

Bruce Johnston

, •

What is the medical term for an ice cream headache, or brain freeze?

Sphenopalatine ganglioneuralgia

What did Redondo Beach, California adopt as the city's official bird in 1983?

Goodyear Blimp

, ·

Sleeping through winter is hibernation, while sleeping through summer is what?

Estivation

, ·

What company did Reed Hastings start after racking up a $40 late fee on a VHS copy of "Apollo 13"?

Netflix

, ·

Who was the official hair consultant to the 1984 Los Angeles Olympics?

Vidal Sussoon

, ·

What is the scientific name for a rabbit's tail?

Scut

Las Vegas blackjack dealers stand on what number?

17

What Major League Baseball team's home field is Minute Maid Park?

Houston Astros

What NFL quarterback predicted a Super Bowl III win?

Joe Namath

What automaker manufactured the Skylark GSX?

Buick

What is Chester Cheetah's brand?

Cheetos

What is Billy Graham's occupation?

Evangelist

What is the Tennessee state fruit?

Tomato

, •

What is the peninsula region of Southeast Europe called?

Balkans

, •

Which US state is nicknamed the Great Lakes State?

Michigan

, •

Where did Red Bull energy drink originate?

Thailand

, •

"Dookie" is the title of an album by what band?

Green Day

, •

What country is home of the Marinara dance?

Peru

What is the Colorado state gemstone?

Aquamarine

, •

What was the pace car for the 1923 Indianapolis 500?

Duesenberg

, •

What was Chevrolet's "pony car" answer to the Ford Mustang?

Camaro

, •

What is the New York state fruit?

Apple

, •

What was Whitey Bulger's profession?

Gangster

, •

What car is a modified Plymouth Road Runner?

Superbird

What is known as the state nut of Oregon?

Hazelnut

, ·

What group launched the careers of guitarists Eric Clapton, Jimmy Page and Jeff Beck?

The Yardbirds

, ·

Which band recorded the 1993 song titled "Cryin'"?

Aerosmith

, ·

What company makes Les Paul guitars?

Gibson

, ·

What are baby frogs are called?

Tadpoles

, ·

What is Kenny Loggins' famous dance movie song?

Footloose

What is Arizona's state gemstone?

Turquoise

, •

What sweet pastry of Viennese origin is a specialty of Denmark?

Danish

, •

What US state is nicknamed the Beaver State?

Oregon

, •

What is Bruce Wayne's alias?

Batman

, •

What is known as a costume or masquerade?

Disguise

, •

What is the California state tree?

Redwood

, •

What king of England was nicknamed the "Conqueror"?

William

, ·

Since 1964, what has been an Olympic martial arts sport?

Judo

, ·

Who performed the 2013 pop song "Wrecking Ball"?

Miley Cyrus

, ·

What is the Vlasic pickles mascot?

A stork

, ·

An enclosed area for musical performances or indoor sports is called what?

Arena

, ·

What NFL team is based in Landover, Maryland?

Redskins

What is the state of Louisiana's nickname?

Pelican State

, ·

What country is the origin of tacos
and quesadillas?

Mexico

, ·

Who was President Jimmy Carter's
Vice President?

Walter Mondale

, ·

The rock band Scorpions formed
where in 1965?

Germany

, ·

What country was named after
the king of Spain?

Philippines

, ·

Food that satisfies Jewish law is called what?

Kosher

What outbreak was traced to Disneyland in 2015?

Measles

, •

What was Zimbabwe once known as?

Rhodesia

, •

In Alaska, what are the Yupik and Inuit known as?

Eskimos

, •

What are the large sacred structures found in Giza, Egypt?

Pyramids

, •

What NBA team is located in Atlanta, Georgia?

Hawks

, •

What is the Nevada state flower?

Sagebrush

What is the largest city of Hawaii?

Honolulu

, ·

What was a 1983 novel by William Kennedy?

Ironweed

, ·

At the 72nd Academy Awards, Robin Williams performed what Oscar-nominated song that had a word censored?

"Blame Canada" (South Park: Bigger, Longer & Uncut)

, ·

What muscle car was made by Plymouth from 1964–1974?

Barracuda

, ·

What medical condition can be defined as excessive uneasiness?

Anxiety

, ·

What automobile was built by Dodge from 1960 to 1976 in North America?

Dart

What company makes Katana motorcycles?

Suzuki

, ·

Where does digestion take place
in a human body?

Stomach

, ·

What is the Major League Baseball team
in Minnesota?

Twins

, ·

What sweet food substance is brown,
powdered, or granulated?

Sugar

, ·

What National Hockey League team is based
in New York City?

Rangers

, ·

Geddy Lee plays bass and sings
in what Canadian trio?

Rush

April 30, 1975, was the fall of what city, ending the Vietnam War?

Saigon

, •

Michael Jackson enlisted Vincent Price to provide a spoken word segment on the title track of what album?

Thriller

, •

Also called sakura, what blossom is a symbol of Japan?

Cherry blossom

, •

What is the Washington state marine mammal?

Orca

, •

In 2002 Sony announced that it would no longer produce video recorders using what format, a rival to VHS?

Betamax

Though the largest primates, they have a smaller relative brain size than chimpanzees?

Gorillas

, .

Covering barely 100 acres, what's the smallest country in Europe?

Vatican

, .

What is a Himalayan goat with backward-curving horns?

Ibex

, .

Paul Simon's 1973 hit begged, "Mama don't let them take what away"?

Kodachrome

, .

At Market Square Arena on June 26, 1977 who gave his last live concert?

Elvis Presley

David Coverdale wondered, "Is This Love" while fronting what group?

Whitesnake

, •

In 1966 this crooner hit No. 1 on the Billboard charts with "Strangers In The Night"?

Frank Sinatra

, •

A winesap is an all-purpose type of what fruit with a glossy red skin?

Apple

, •

Robert Moog became a household name for the invention of what instrument that bears his name?

Synthesizer

, •

What freshwater crustaceans resemble small lobsters?

Crawfish

Lucas Oil Stadium is this home of what National Football League team?

Indianapolis Colts

' ·

A spirometer is used to measure the air capacity of what?

Lungs

' ·

What are Bowler hats worn in Bolivia called?

Bombin

' ·

With ancestors as big as elephants, what slow beasts now just hang upside down in trees?

Sloth

' ·

John Elway was quarterback of this team from 1983 to 1998?

Denver Broncos

' ·

Who was awarded the Nobel Prize for his work with penicillin in 1928?

Alexander Fleming

What African nation is home of about 10 million people, and Victoria Falls?

Zambia

, .

Frosty the Snowman had a corncob pipe and a button nose and two eyes made out of what?

Coal

, .

The Strait of Gibraltar separates what country from Spain by about 8 miles?

Morocco

, .

In May 1927 what American aviator became the first man to fly the Atlantic solo?

Charles Lindbergh

, .

John Madden coached what team to victory in Super Bowl XI?

Oakland Raiders

, .

A card player's stake is called what?

Ante

Aerodynamic friction force, or clothing associated with cross-dressing is called what?

Drag

, ·

What is the USA's largest man-made reservoir, created by Hoover Dam?

Lake Mead

, ·

What team's 1991 NBA championship was the first in the club's 25-year history?

Chicago Bulls

, ·

What goober accounts for about one-sixth of the world's vegetable oil production?

Peanuts

, ·

For what purpose was bubble wrap created?

Wallpaper

, ·

The University of Alabama team nickname is what?

Crimson Tide

Who played lead guitar on Led Zeppelin's "Stairway to Heaven"?

Jimmy Page

, •

Terrence Howard plays music magnate Lucious Lyon in what series?

Empire

, •

What is the noisy landmark at the northern end of London's Houses of Parliament?

Big Ben

, •

Artistic forms of the Google logo are called what?

Doodles

, •

What NFL team won Super Bowl XLVIII in 2014?

Seattle Seahawks

Led Zeppelin called it quits in 1980 after the death of what drummer?

John Bonham

, •

What state was the site of half of the major battles in the US Civil War?

Virginia

, •

In 2015, the United States reestablished diplomatic relations with what country, 90 miles south of Key West?

Cuba

, •

What dinosaur is Colorado's state fossil?

Stegosaurus

, •

What disc jockey is often credited with coining the term "rock 'n' roll"?

Alan Freed

What is a type of hickory nut, popular for pralines and pies?

Pecan

, ·

A silhouetted, bow tie-wearing bunny is the logo for what magazine?

Playboy

, ·

The Loma Prieta earthquake postponed Game 3 of the 1989 World Series between the San Francisco Giants and what team?

Oakland Athletics

, ·

What is Hawaii's state bird?

Nene

, ·

As Saul, Saint Paul heard the voice of Jesus while on the road to what city?

Damascus

What is the capital of the African country of Burkina Faso?

Ouagadougou

, •

Gillette Stadium is home to what NFL franchise?

New England Patriots

, •

Pittsburgh is home to what NFL team?

Steelers

, •

With about 100,000 people, Billings is what state's most populous city?

Montana

, •

A crude representation or a statue or model of a disliked person is called what?

Effigy

, •

What vehicle was pioneered by Igor Sikorsky in 1939?

Helicopter

The Forbidden City is at the heart of what capital city?

Beijing, China

, •

American football is a sport played by two teams of how many players?

Eleven

, •

Who are the five original members of Aerosmith?

Brad Whitford, Joey Kramer, Tom Hamilton, Joe Perry & Steven Tyler

, •

What game involves careful extraction of plastic body parts including the Adam's apple, broken heart, and funny bone?

Operation

, •

Mel Blanc's voice brought what duck to life?

Daffy Duck

In 2000 what Minnesota team joined
the National Hockey League?

Minnesota Wild

, .

What toy company builds more cars
than Ford, GM & Chrysler combined?

Mattel

, .

For about 6 million years, the Colorado River
has been eroding rock, creating what?

Grand Canyon

, .

The largest of what bird in the United States
is called pileated?

Woodpecker

, .

Who is the only NFL player
that can be sacked?

Quarterback

The willingness of Tennessee's citizens to serve in the military earned the state this nickname?

Volunteer State

, ·

What bird's name comes from its ability to copy the songs of other birds?

Mockingbird

, ·

What is Nevada's state mineral?

Silver

, ·

In the southeastern part of Ontario lies what city, the capital of Canada?

Ottawa

, ·

What was Ellis Island used for from 1892-1954?

Immigration

Originally, the green 'Life Saver' in the classic roll of 5 flavors was lime; today, it's what flavor?

Watermelon

, ·

Croutons or bread crumbs mixed with sage is stuffed in the cavity of what bird for Thanksgiving?

Turkey

, ·

What red-hot, pungent powder are made from various tropical chiles originated in French Guiana?

Cayenne

, ·

What are units that measure the intensity of sound?

Decibel

, ·

What American professional basketball team is based in New Orleans, Louisiana?

Pelicans

What is the Wisconsin state motto, meaning to proceed?

Forward

, ·

In a June 1987 speech, Reagan challenged Gorbachev to tear down what wall?

Berlin Wall

, ·

What is Michigan's state fossil?

Mastodon

, ·

In 1984, what company's DynaTac mobile phone sold for $4,000?

Motorola

, ·

What is the state mineral of Utah?

Copper

, ·

Some say UFOs landed in what New Mexico city in 1947?

Roswell

What is the University of Texas football team called?

Longhorns

, ·

What title is granted to a squire by a monarch?

Knight

, ·

No longer "falling down", London Bridge is now found where?

Lake Havasu City, Arizona

, ·

What team won Super Bowl XXXV, beating the Giants 34-7?

Baltimore Ravens

, ·

What dinosaur is known & named for its 3 horns?

Triceratops

, ·

What African country is the origin of Makossa music?

Cameroon

Bordering China, what country
is also called Burma?

Myanmar

, •

Who was the 2nd & 4th President of Russia?

Vladimir Putin

, •

Named for England's leading industrial city,
what is Alabama's leading industrial city?

Birmingham

, •

What country led the boycott of the 1984
Summer Olympics in Los Angeles?

Soviet Union

, •

University of Wisconsin sports
use what nickname?

Badgers

, •

Who was the first US president
to serve 8 full years?

Thomas Jefferson

What is the most populous city in Ohio?

Cleveland

, .

What actress moves from the city to the suburbs in "Confessions of a Teenage Drama Queen"?

Lindsay Lohan

, .

What lake borders Toledo, Ohio?

Lake Erie

, .

What sport is also called wickets?

Croquet

, .

What is Nebraska's state tree?

Cottonwood

, .

Who are the NFL team that plays at AT&T Stadium in in Arlington, Texas?

Dallas Cowboys

What is Cleveland's NBA team?

Cavaliers

, .

What is the state flower of Indiana?

Peony

, .

In 1971, what San Diego NBA team moved to Houston?

Rockets

, .

Who was the 43rd United States president?

George W. Bush

, .

The wild variety of what grain is actually a type of marsh grass native to the Great Lakes region?

Rice

, .

Adam & Eve lived in a garden, where?

Eden

, •

Where did Apollo 11 land in 1969?

Moon

, •

Seven colors are traditionally identified in one of what?

Rainbow

, •

What is the scientific term for an Egg-laying mammal?

Monotremata

, •

Tomato and Chicken Noodle are popular flavors of what?

Soup

, •

What NBA team shares the Staples Center with the Los Angeles Lakers?

Clippers

According to legend, what Italian princess had a pizza named after her?

Margherita of Savoy

, •

What is the most common wildcat in North America?

Bobcat

, •

In 2014, the city of Calgary, Alberta, Canada set the world record for most people dressed as what?

Batman (542 caped crusaders)

, •

1 in 5,000 north Atlantic lobsters are born what color?

Bright blue

, •

A million of what can be created from a cord of wood?

Toothpicks

A 41-gun salute is the traditional salute to a royal birth in what country?

England

, •

What game was originally denounced by critics as "sex in a box"?

Twister

, •

What mammal holds hands while sleeping to stay together?

Sea otters

, •

What former NFL star was originally cast to play the Terminator in the 1984 film?

O.J. Simpson

, •

What 2016 US presidential candidate owns a bottled water brand?

Donald Trump (Trump Natural Spring Water)

, •

What store was founded in 1962 in Arkansas?

Wal-Mart

What band has changed their original lineup 22 times since forming in 1985?

Guns N' Roses

, •

In 1930, what was discovered by astronomer Clyde Tombaugh?

Pluto

, •

What famous race horse born in Kentucky never ran a race there?

Man o' War

, •

More than 120 nationalities are represented in what country, the world's largest landlocked country by land area?

Kazakhstan

, •

What carnivorous plant is native to North Carolina?

Venus Fly Trap

The first commercial oil well in the United States was tapped in what state in 1859?

Pennsylvania

, •

What dance, known as the "dance of love" was invented in Argentina?

Tango

, •

During the 1943 National Football League season, what two teams merged temporarily to form one team?

The Pittsburgh Steelers and the Philadelphia Eagles (Steagles)

, •

To defend the frontier from Indians and dangerous outlaws, what law enforcement agency was founded in Texas in 1835?

Rangers

, •

In 1955, who took part in the first televised press conference?

President Dwight Eisenhower

What song became a theme of hope during the Iranian hostage crisis from 1979-1981?

Tie a Yellow Ribbon Round the Ole Oak Tree (Dawn featuring Tony Orlando)

, •

Tulips were not first grown in Holland, but where?

Turkey

, •

Who was the 1992 gold medalist boxer known as "The Golden Boy"?

Oscar De La Hoya

, •

In the 1940s Richard James worked on a set of springs to stabilize items in rough seas; that became what toy in 1945?

Slinky

, •

What 2016 presidential candidate co-wrote the political memoir titled "Outsider in the White House"?

Bernie Sanders

Known as the "Great American Race", what has been the traditional opening race for the NASCAR Sprint Cup series since 1982?

Daytona 500

, .

1968 brought the first major-brand sneakers with what brand name fastener instead of laces?

Velcro

, .

On March 16, 1974 what president played piano at the dedication of the Grand Ole Opry House in Nashville?

Richard Nixon

, .

What Georgia city was first known as Terminus, and later "Marthasville" to honor the Governor's daughter?

Atlanta

, .

In Sweden what patron saint is honored on December 13 as part of the Christmas celebration?

St. Lucy

1965 saw the first manned flight in what 2-man NASA program?

Gemini

, ·

What name is given to the NASA robotic rover on planet Mars?

Curiosity

, ·

Costa Rica has coasts on what 2 bodies of water?

It features 800 miles of coastline, both on the Atlantic and Pacific Oceans.

, ·

What city has the world's largest concentration of water parks all in one area?

Wisconsin Dells, Wisconsin

, ·

What falls off the human body after two to three months in space?

Skin calluses on feet

What was discovered in Arkansas by John W. Huddleston in 1906?

Diamonds

, •

Humans have the same amount of hair follicles as what?

Chimpanzees

, •

Months that begin on a Sunday always have what?

Friday the 13th

, •

According to the CIA, the literacy rate is 100% in what country?

North Korea

, •

Yale University scientists suggest that the exoplanet called "55 Cancri e" is covered in what?

Diamonds

What American advertising mascot was invented in New Mexico after the Capitan Gap fire of 1950?

Smokey the Bear

, .

What children's stories were inspired by a black bear who was exported from Canada to the London Zoo in 1915?

Winnie-the-Pooh

, .

A monstrous hurricane in 1900 nearly wiped what Texas city off the map?

Galveston

, .

There are about 52 species of what type of bird in Costa Rica?

Hummingbirds

, .

What website features an average of $680 worth of transactions every second?

Ebay

Ayatollah Khomeini was what country's political & religious leader from 1979-1989?

Iran

, .

At the beginning of World War I, how were British tanks grouped?

Tanks had genders. The male tanks had cannons attached while the females carried machine guns.

, .

What creature can change its sex multiple times through its life?

Oysters

, .

What explorer is regarded as the first European to set foot on the shores of North America?

Leif Eriksson

, .

Invisible ink can be made by mixing 2 oz. of water with 1 oz. of what Arm & Hammer product?

Baking soda

The term Hoosier most commonly refers to a person from what U.S. State?

Indiana

, •

What state had the first town named for Lincoln--in 1853, before he was even president?

Illinois

, •

Who served as co-captains of the 1992 United States men's Olympic basketball team, known as the "Dream Team"?

Magic Johnson and Larry Bird

, •

What constellation is seen on the Alaska state flag?

Big Dipper

, •

What country has fought for freedom in insurrections 43 times from 1600 to 1945?

Poland

The Battle of the Little Bighorn, also called Custer's Last Stand, took place in what state?

Montana

, ·

Also the hometown of Bill Clinton, what town claims to be the watermelon capital of the world?

Hope, Arkansas

, ·

The technical term for the Northern lights is what?

Aurora Borealis

, ·

What is the largest nation that doesn't border an ocean?

Kazakhstan

, ·

The Lumiere brothers unveiled the world's first commercial movie screening in what city in 1895?

Paris, France

Not a perfect sphere, what is the actual shape of planet Earth?

It's actually an oblate spheroid, thanks to a slight equatorial bulge.

, .

Of Austria's 9 states, what is the smallest in area?

Vienna

, .

North Carolina is the largest producer of what botanical product?

Tobacco

, .

The shortest war on record lasted 38 minutes in 1896 & involved what countries?

United Kingdom and Zanzibar

, .

The first cartoon characters associated with a Kellogg's product were what in the early 1930s?

Snap, Crackle, and Pop

What country's official currency
is called forint?

Hungary

, •

What English settlement was founded by Sir Walter Raleigh in what is now North Carolina?

Roanoke Colony

, •

Darwin, Minnesota is the home
of what roadside attraction?

World's Largest Twine Ball

, •

During World War II, the crew of the British submarine HMS Trident kept what aboard their vessel for six weeks?

A fully grown reindeer called Pollyanna (It was a gift from Russia)

, •

The geographic center of the European Union is in what country?

Germany

According to the World Wildlife Fund, half of what has disappeared since 1970?

All animals

, .

Who does lawn mowing at Google headquarters in Mountain View, California?

Google HQ rents goats from California Grazing to mow their lawns and fields.

, .

32 million what call every inch of your skin home?

Bacteria

, .

What river is mentioned most often in the Bible?

Jordan

, .

What organization banked over 13 million units of blood for plasma by the end of WWII?

Red Cross

What is a Tibetan ox used to carry travelers and mail called?

Yak

, •

What colorful company was formerly known as Binney & Smith?

Crayola

, •

What is a more common name for the Watch Tower Bible and Tract Society?

Jehovah's Witnesses

, •

The Ancient Greeks believed gods and goddesses lived above specially protected golden clouds on top of where?

Mount Olympus

, •

What is a popular destination for tight-rope walkers & honeymooners?

Niagara Falls

"Call me Ishmael" was the opening line in what classic novel?

Moby Dick

, .

The United States captured all of what territory from the Spanish by 1821?

Florida

, .

Snakes have no arms or legs but can have 600 of what in their flexible spine?

Vertebrae

, .

What is the name of the main character in "The Hunchback of Notre-Dame"?

Quasimodo

, .

What disaster in 1937 marked the end of the use of airships for commercial air transportation?

Hindenburg

What actor has played or voiced "The Incredible Hulk" in every live action incarnation since 1978?

Lou Ferrigno

, ·

Vlad the Impaler, or Dracula was born in what country?

Transylvania

, ·

In the U.S. what holiday is celebrated the third Sunday in June?

Father's Day

, ·

What was the first religion to teach monotheism, or the doctrine of one god?

Judaism

, ·

In 1979 debris from what space station fell from orbit & dropped into the Indian Ocean?

Skylab

There's a pyramid on the back of what U.S. denomination?

One-dollar bill

, .

Anne Sullivan spelled out lectures in what woman's hand, helping her to graduate with honors in 1904?

Helen Keller

, .

Before the euro, the drachma was the currency of what country?

Greece

, .

Where is the largest Hindu temple in the world?

Angkor, Cambodia (Angkor Wat)

, .

How many dimples are in an average golf ball?

The average golf ball has 336 dimples

The 1903 World Series between Boston and Pittsburgh was played in how many games?

It was a nine-game series

, •

Who is the head of the Yellow Hat order of Tibetan Buddhists?

Dalai Lama

, •

What is the only continent that does not have land areas below sea level?

Antarctica

, •

What chambered muscular organ pumps blood?

Heart

, •

A reclining Buddha, 49 feet high, can be found at the Wat Pho temple in what city?

Bangkok

The word "Checkmate" in chess comes from the Persian phrase "Shah Mat," which means what?

The king is dead

, ·

What is a common name for the tympanic membrane?

Eardrum

, ·

Nicknamed "Little Sure Shot", who was with Buffalo Bill's Wild West Show for 17 years?

Annie Oakley

, ·

In 1537, who declared February 14 the holiday of St. Valentine's Day?

King Henry VII

, ·

The underside of a horse's hoof is called what?

A frog

The Chalet Cheese Cooperative in Monroe, Wisconsin is the only American company that produces what type of smelly cheese?

Limburger

, ·

A group of owls is called what?

A parliament

, ·

What is the science of sound called?

Acoustics

, ·

What was the first coin minted in the United States?

A silver dollar

, ·

Beelzebub, another name for the devil, is Hebrew for what?

Lord of the Flies

, ·

Centuries before Crest or Colgate, what did ancient Romans use as toothpaste?

Crushed mouse brains

What state is nicknamed "The Old Dominion"?

Virginia

, .

What liquid can be used as a substitute for blood plasma?

Coconut water

, .

What is the substance that allows you to blow a bubble with bubble gum?

Rubber

, .

In times before the use of indoor plumbing, what symbols came to represent male and female outhouses?

The half-moon and the star

, .

What is your fear if you've got Pteronophobia?

Fear of being tickled by feathers

, .

What animal secretes its own red sunscreen when it becomes hot?

Hippopotamus

What device was invented in 1881 by dentist Alfred P. Southwick?

Electric chair

, •

A shrimp's heart is located where?

In its head

, •

On his famous transatlantic flight, what did Charles Lindbergh bring to eat?

Four sandwiches

, •

What is the ingredient in lipstick that makes lips reflect light?

Fish scales

, •

What animals have three eyelids for protection from blowing sand?

Camels

Who once broke out of a Crown Point, Indiana jail with a gun made of wood and shoe polish?

John Dillinger

, .

Mount Olympus Mons on Mars is three times the size of what mountain?

Mount Everest

, .

What percentage of people who use personal ads for dating are already married?

Thirty-five percent

, .

Clocks are typically not found on the walls of what?

Casinos

, .

Just a few ounces of what can kill a small sized dog?

Chocolate

In 1865 what amendment to the Constitution abolished slavery in the U.S.?

13th Amendment

, •

What was the first book published in C.S. Lewis' "Chronicles of Narnia"?

The Lion, the Witch and the Wardrobe

, •

The high school set used in "Buffy the Vampire Slayer" was the same set used in what series?

Beverly Hills, 90210

, •

In Scotland, April Fool's Day is often called what?

Hunt the Gowk Day

, •

Medbox company is the maker of one of the world's first vending machines of what product?

Marijuana

Located on Bennelong Point in Port Jackson Harbour, What Australian landmark's roof has been described as sails?

Sydney Opera House

, .

What was Randy Newman's Oscar-nominated song from "Toy Story"?

You've Got a Friend in Me

, .

What is the classic naval combat game from Milton Bradley?

Battleship

, .

What was the United States Forest Service's Woodsy Owl's tagline?

"Give a hoot — don't pollute!"

, .

What nation's flag is red, black and white with two green stars?

Syria

What military vehicle was marketed commercially in 1992?

Hummer

, ·

What action figure was named after a 1945 WWII movie?

GI. Joe

, ·

The animated series "Ren & Stimpy" introduced what catchy song?

Happy Happy Joy Joy

, ·

What character was famous for busting through the walls of thirsty children?

Kool-Aid Man

, ·

What group made the most appearances on "The Ed Sullivan Show"?

Dave Clark Five

In 1981, what country became the last nation on the American mainland to gain independence?

Belize

, ·

Why did President Anwar Sadat of Egypt get the 1978 Nobel Peace Prize?

For a Peace Treaty with Israel

, ·

What song features these words: "I was dreamin' when I wrote this so sue me if I go 2 fast"?

1999 (Prince)

, ·

In 1997, after a thirty year drought, what team won Super Bowl XXXI?

Green Bay Packers

, ·

What term is used to denote the terrestrial stage of the development of the young newt?

Eft

Fill in the blanks: In Revelation 1:8, the Lord said, "I Am the ,.__&,.__"?

Alpha & Omega

, .

Who proved lightning is electricity in 1752?

Ben Franklin

, .

Richard Bachman is a pen name used by what horror fiction author?

Stephen King

, .

Candice Bergen's character in what sitcom gave up drinking after a stay at the Betty Ford Clinic?

Murphy Brown

, .

As Russell Hammond, Billy Crudup said "I am a golden god!" in what film?

Almost Famous

On Valentine's Day, 1991, what "Sleepless in Seattle" star married her sweetheart, Dennis Quaid?

Meg Ryan

, .

"Show Me The Way" & "Do You Feel Like We Do" are featured on what artist's 1976 live album?

Peter Frampton

, .

The Blackberry Storm was competing with what Apple branded product?

iPhone

, .

In 1980 Reykjavik Theater director VIgdis Finnbogadottir became what country's first woman president?

Iceland

, .

On September 28, 2014, what 40 year old Yankees shortstop played his last game, to cheers in Boston?

Derek Jeter

What was J.K. Rowling's third Harry Potter novel, released in 1999?

Harry Potter and the Prisoner of Azkaban

, •

Gordon Freeman is the main character of what video game series?

Half Life

, •

In Australia, what tall flowering trees provide oil for medicine & leaves for koalas?

Eucalyptus

, •

The Weather Channel website has a section for allergy sufferers that list "hot spots" for what?

Pollen

, •

David Spade's first big-screen role was in "Citizens on Patrol", the fourth film in what series?

Police Academy

What stock car driver died in 2001 due to injuries suffered during the Daytona 500?

Dale Earnhardt

, .

What band's "Viva la Vida" album cover featured Delacroix' 1830 painting "Liberty Leading the People"?

Coldplay

, .

Lebanon banned what 2003 novel that suggests Jesus was a dad?

The Da Vinci Code (Dan Brown)

, .

In 1978 what Cincinnati Reds player set a modern-day National League record with a 44-game hitting streak?

Pete Rose

, .

What team won the first World Series to be played indoors in 1987?

Minnesota Twins

2 translators of what man's "The Satanic Verses" novel were brutally attacked in July 1991?

Salman Rushdie

, .

Who is Batman's love interest in the video game "Batman: Arkham City"?

Seline Kyle, Catwoman

, .

The box variety of what cnidarian kills its prey with some of the strongest venom in the world?

Jellyfish

, .

What PBS series was once hosted by Bob Vila?

This Old House

, .

Who won an Oscar Award for "As Good As It Gets" and an Emmy Award for "Mad About You"?

Helen Hunt

What system for informing people about abductions is named for an unfortunate 9-year-old?

Amber Alert System

, •

Former mortuary science student Jonathan Davis plays bagpipes & sings for what group?

Korn

, •

What Egyptian deity's name is not so popular now that it is the same as a Mideast terrorist group?

Isis

, •

What celebrity couple announced their first pregnancy on Instagram January 31, 2015?

Justin Timberlake and wife Jessica Biel

, •

What quarterback retired after his Denver Broncos defeated the Atlanta Falcons, 34-19 In Super Bowl XXXIII?

John Elway

What 1989 movie did Barack Obama take Michelle to see on their first date?

Do the Right Thing

, ·

What was the first space shuttle that could lift off like a rocket & land like a plane?

Columbia

, ·

What 1998 remake had this tagline: "Check in. Unpack. Relax. Take a shower"?

Psycho

, ·

Former Miss South Dakota Mary Hart was best known as a host of what gossip program?

Entertainment Tonight

, ·

Heather O' Rourke proclaims: "They're heeere!" in what film?

Poltergeist

"Moonwalk" was the title of whose 1988 autobiography?

Michael Jackson

, ·

Justin Timberlake appears on what album, clad in a tuxedo, getting his eyes examined?

The 20/20 Experience

, ·

An accident at what power station produced a radioactive cloud more than 3,000 feet high in April 1986?

Chernobyl

, ·

What couple's "General Hospital" wedding was the big one of 1981?

Luke & Laura

, ·

In 2013 what driver became a 6-time NASCAR champion, winning the Sprint Cup Series title by 19 points?

Jimmie Johnson

"Lost World" was what author's sequel to "Jurassic Park"?

Michael Crichton

, •

What musical instrument simulation game has a working whammy bar?

Guitar Hero

, •

In April 1992 Los Angeles erupted in riots after 4 policemen were acquitted of beating what man?

Rodney King

, •

Kate Walsh played Dr. Addison Montgomery in what series, a spinoff from "Grey's Anatomy"?

Private Practice

, •

What 2009 Quentin Tarantino film was set during World War II?

Inglourious Basterds

What famous line was used by Mrs. Fletcher in a LifeCall commercial?

I've fallen and I can't get up

, •

Who sings the song "Hips Don't Lie", featuring Wyclef Jean?

Shakira

, •

Jim Carrey voiced the title pachyderm that discovers voices coming from a speck of dust in what film?

Dr. Seuss' Horton Hears a Who!

, •

What singer shaved off her hair in 2007?

Britney Spears

, •

What Red Sox legend's family had legal battles over what to do with his body after his death in 2002?

Ted Williams

What author wrote the Jason Bourne novels, beginning with "The Bourne Identity"?

Robert Ludlum

, •

What is the goal in the video game 1942?

Destroy the entire Japanese air fleet

, •

Who was best known for singing Ricky Martin's song "She Bangs" on American Idol in 2004?

William Hung

, •

What icon of extended battery life has been going & going since 1989?

The Energizer Bunny

, •

Dave Chappelle played the character named Ahchoo in what 1993 comedy?

Robin Hood: Men in Tights

, •

What is the multimedia tablet called "Fire"?

Amazon Kindle

The word 'anorexia' entered the American vocabulary after what singer died of heart failure in 1983?

Karen Carpenter

, ·

What ex-preacher turned stand-up comic was sadly killed in an auto accident in 1992?

Sam Kinison

, ·

People who get aroused by touching animal skin, fur or leather have what condition?

Hyphephilia

, ·

On December 30, 2006, what dictator was executed in Baghdad?

Saddam Hussein

, ·

On November 20, 1985, what product did Bill Gates of Microsoft introduce?

Microsoft Windows 1.0

King Pig is the lazy overlord of what game you can play on your smartphone?

Angry Birds

, .

In 2013, McDonald's restaurants cut their 40 year relationship with what company?

Heinz Ketchup

, .

In a June 1987 speech, who challenged: "Mr. Gorbachev, tear down this wall."?

Ronald Reagan

, .

What did Apple co-founder Steve Jobs wish to call the Macintosh?

Apple Bicycle

, .

In December 2001, what company filed the largest corporate bankruptcy in U.S. history?

Enron

, .

What is Burger King called in Australia?

Hungry Jack's

Who was Time Magazine's person of the year of 2006?

You (all World Wide Web users)

, .

When Israel's first president, Chaim Weizmann, died, who was offered the position, but refused?

Alfred Einstein

, .

The glue on postage stamps of what country is kosher?

Israel

, .

Where is Hawaii 2?

Hawaii 2 is a private 6-acre island located in St. George Lake near the town of Liberty, Maine.

, .

The fat and jolly Santa Claus we know today was originally created for what company's ad campaign?

Coca-Cola

What new born animal stands at around 6 feet tall?

Giraffe

, ·

What unofficial September 5th holiday was conceived in Bedford, Massachusetts in 2000?

International Bacon Day

, ·

Bayer, the makers of aspirin, introduced what as a cough medicine?

Heroin

, ·

When traveling in groups, what animals breathe in unison?

Orcas (Killer whales)

, ·

Paul Hunn holds the record for the loudest burp, which was 118.1 decibels, which is as loud as what?

A chainsaw

The modern civil rights movement began in 1955 when Rosa Parks did what?

She refused to give up her seat on an Alabama bus

, ·

What sports equipment has reached speeds of up to 150 miles per hour?

Pucks hit by hockey sticks

, ·

Hershey's makes one million miles of what candy every year?

Twizzlers

, ·

37 different animals have been featured in what product since 1903?

Barnum's Animals Crackers

, ·

What nation is only about 50 miles from Florida?

Bahamas

Chemical compounds that are made up of oxygen, hydrogen and carbon are called what?

Carbohydrates

, .

What roller coaster at Six Flags Magic Mountain in California, goes from 0 to 100 miles per hour in only 7 seconds?

Superman: Escape from Krypton

, .

The male sex cells of flowering plants are carried to the female cells via what?

Pollen

, .

"Bear" sometimes follows the name of what Aussie mammal that's actually 100% marsupial?

Koala

, .

What country sits between Egypt and Algeria in Northwestern Africa?

Libya

What bridge in Istanbul, Turkey spans two continents?

The Bosphorus Bridge

, .

What human cells have no nucleus and do not contain genetic information?

Red blood cells

, .

According to the Boat Owners Association of the United States, what was the most popular boat name in 2002?

Liberty

, .

What is the only letter not found on the periodic table of elements?

The letter "J" is the only one not found on the periodic table

, .

The Aztecs used what as currency?

Cocoa beans

What hand is considered unclean in Muslim cultures?

The left hand is considered to be unclean

, .

Despite its name, the Equator does not run through what African country?

Equatorial Guinea

, .

The dodo was last observed on what Indian Ocean island, 500 miles east of Madagascar?

Mauritius

, .

What is the chief cash crop of Palau?

Coconuts

, .

Bulgaria, Greece, and Yugoslavia share the region of what ancient country today?

Macedonia

, .

For more than 3,000 years, what insects have been used to close wounds in India, Asia and

South America?

Carpenter ants

, ·

What country has the largest number of butterfly species in the world?

Nigeria

, ·

What is the planned world's first carbon free city in United Arab Emirates to be called?

Masdar City

, ·

"We Shall Overcome" was a popular anthem of what campaign?

Civil Rights Movement

, ·

In 1905 biologist Nettie Stevens showed that what 2 chromosomes determine a person's sex?

The X and Y chromosomes

, ·

French soldiers during World War I had what nickname?

Poilu (Hairy one)

What nation used to create pots in the shape of peanuts that were highly prized?

Inca

' •

What animal breeds so quickly that in just 18 months, 2 of them could produce over 1 million relatives?

Rats

' •

Due to religious reasons, what city is encircled by a constantly maintained, continuous string of clear wire?

Manhattan

' •

What company's advertisements were known for the quote "Can you hear me now?"

Verizon Wireless

' •

Santa Anna was the Mexican army commander at the battle of what San Antonio mission?

The Alamo

A baby is born every 2 seconds
in what country?

India

, •

Why was the XBOX logo green?

Coworkers took every other color marker the artist had

, •

What 'out of this world' course is offered at The Rochester Institute of Technology in New York?

Space Tourism

, •

Amsterdam Vallon and Bill the Butcher are the main characters of what 2002 film?

Gangs of New York

, •

Until his untimely death from a stingray's barb, who was director of the Australia Zoo in Queensland?

Steve Irwin

In the 1980s Johnny Gilbert was the announcer on the $20,000 version of what Dick Clark-hosted game show?

The $20,000 Pyramid

/ •

What late December celebration was created by Professor Maulana Karenga in 1965?

Kwanzaa

/ •

A headband with springs carrying ornaments, sometimes bunny ears, is called what?

Deely bobber

/ •

British Airways retired its fleet of what supersonic jet in 2003?

Concorde

/ •

During 1984-1990 Canadian teams won the NHL Stanley Cup seven straight years with what team winning five of those Championships?

Edmonton Oilers

In a 2013 interview with Oprah, who finally admitted to using performance-enhancing drugs to win the Tour de France?

Lance Armstrong

, .

Who got his big break starring in the 1960s TV sitcom, "I Spy"?

Bill Cosby

, .

What was the "12/12/12 Concert" in response to?

It was a benefit concert for Hurricane Sandy victims

, .

Operation Desert Shield was the buildup to the 1991 military offensive against Iraq that was called what operation?

Desert Storm

, .

What "bug" was supposed to hit at the end of 1999?

Y2K

What actor crash landed an airplane on a golf course in March 2015?

Harrison Ford

, ·

What injury sidelined Green Bay Packers quarterback Aaron Rodgers until week 17 of the 2013 season?

Left collarbone

, ·

What dog breed won at the 139th Westminster Kennel Club Dog Show in February 2015?

Beagle

, ·

What British king was reburied after being discovered under a carpark in 2012?

Richard III

, ·

As the top goal scorer of Brazil 2014, the Golden Boot was awarded to what player?

James Rodriguez (Colombia)

James Earl Ray was best known for assassinating what civil rights leader in 1968?

Martin Luther King, Jr.

, .

What American electronics chain filed for bankruptcy protection in February 2015?

Radio Shack

, .

Who founded Scientology?

L. Ron Hubbard

, .

In what city did riots occur after the death of Freddie Gray, while in police custody?

Baltimore

, .

What Atlanta Braves pitcher finished the 2013 season with an MLB best 50 saves?

Jim Johnson

120 armed members of what group were arrested by U.S. Marshals in 1973 in South Dakota?

American Indian Movement

, .

Temples of Baha'i Faith are required to be in what shape?

Nonagon

, .

What country has 8 of the world's 10 highest peaks?

Nepal

, .

What is the Miami Heat's senior citizen dance squad called?

The Golden Oldies

, .

In 1978, Harvey Milk kicked off his political career by doing what?

He sponsored a pooper-scooper law in San Francisco

The absence of belief in any Gods or spiritual beings is known as what?

Atheism

, •

As per the Worldwide Cost of Living Survey, what is the most expensive city in the world?

Singapore

, •

In 2016, what actor signed 77 new Special Edition Firebird Trans Am Bandits?

Burt Reynolds

, •

LeBron James had a cameo in what 2015 American film?

Trainwreck

, •

What former NFL star shot himself in the leg and was charged with criminal possession of a weapon in 2008?

Plaxico Burress

Who is responsible for the safety of the Pope in Vatican City?

Swiss Guard

, •

What food poisoning bacteria is named after the scientist who identified it, not a fish?

Salmonella

, •

"Iceman" was what Formula One driver's nickname?

Kimi Raikkonen

, •

Who was the former Penn State football coach sentenced to prison for sexual abuse?

Jerry Sandusky

, •

What name is used for the robes that Roman Catholic priests wear?

Cassock

In 2004 the Centers for Disease Control and Prevention announced that what infection had been eliminated from the United States?

Rubella (German measles)

, .

After winning the 2014 FedEx Championship, what golfer deposited $11.44 million into his account and got home in time to witness the birth of his baby girl?

Billy Horschel

, .

Who was the Long Island Lolita that turned violent when Joey Buttafuoco turned her away?

Amy Fisher

, .

Effective January 1, 2015, what did the state of New York ban?

Photography with big cats

, .

Michael Vick's NFL career was derailed when he served time in prison for what in 2007?

Illegal dog fighting

Amid accusations of cheating, the New England Patriots beat what team in Super Bowl XLIX?

Seattle Seahawks

, •

According to a popular rhyme, who 'took an axe and gave her mother forty whacks'?

Lizzie Borden

, •

As planned, what planet did NASA's MESSENGER spacecraft impact on April 30, 2015?

Mercury

, •

After the capture of John Dillinger, which criminal was named "Public Enemy Number One"?

Charles "Pretty Boy" Floyd

, •

Dzhokhar Tsarnaev was sentenced to death in 2015 for planting bombs at what 2013 event?

Boston Marathon

In 1997 what fashion designer known for his "Flash & Trash" chic was slain in front of his Miami Beach mansion?

Gianni Versace

, .

Revealed in March 2015, what did the Polar Remotely Operated Vehicle help study?

Monsoons

, .

What American electronics chain filed for bankruptcy protection in February 2015?

Radio Shack

, .

In 1931 Al Capone got 11 years not for murder or bootlegging but for what?

Tax evasion

, .

Convicted of 33 murders, John Wayne Gacy was known by what nickname?

The Killer Clown

What company acknowledged 11 accidents with its autonomous car?

Google

, .

What country killed over 200,000 people for opposing their government?

Syria

, .

What NASCAR driver won the 2015 Daytona 500?

Joey Logano

, .

What NASA spacecraft became the first to visit a dwarf planet?

Dawn

, .

What nation was created due to the ongoing Croatia-Serbia border dispute?

Liberland

Which Ohio team won the 2015 College Football Championship game?

Ohio State Buckeyes

, ·

What HBO docu-series helped bring down Robert Durst after he seemingly confessed to murder in the finale?

The Jinx

, ·

Players of what sport run an average of 7-9 miles in a game?

Soccer

, ·

The only 2 animals can see completely behind themselves without turning their heads are what?

Rabbit and the parrot

, ·

What Paris landmark has a secret apartment hidden within its highest level?

The Eiffel Tower

What San Francisco 49ers player was slated to play the role of Mary's secret love in "There's Something About Mary"?

Steve Young

, ·

In 1973, TIME Magazine coined what term to describe Rex Humbard's profession?

Televangelism

, ·

What is the shortest complete sentence in the English language?

Go.

, ·

How many miles of telephone wire are strung across the United States?

1,525,000,000 miles

, ·

What is the only English word ending in "mt"?

Dreamt

How many pieces of mail are delivered each year in the U.S.?

166,875,000,000 pieces of mail

, .

In a high speed chase, what percentage of people typically gets away from police in Los Angeles?

18% of people

, .

2013 was the first year since 1987 to feature what?

Four different numbers

, .

How many people attend Major League baseball games each year?

56,000,000 people

, .

How much paper is used each year in the U.S.?

85,000,000 tons

, .

A cat has how many muscles in each ear?

32 muscles

What animal's jaw cannot move sideways?

A cat

, •

Because it contains the element phosphorus, what animal's urine glows under a black light?

Cat urine

, •

What comedian once asked the children who watched his show to send him "funny green pieces of paper with pictures of U.S. Presidents" from their parents' wallets and purses?

Soupy Sales

, •

What insect will live nine days without its head before it starves to death?

A cockroach

, •

A company in Taiwan makes dinnerware out of what material?

Wheat, so you can eat your plate!

The first computer for business use was built by Cambridge mathematician John Simmons to do what?

Add up the receipts of iced buns

, •

What percent of New York City cab drivers are recent immigrants?

84% of NYC cabbies

, •

If Barbie were life-size, what would her measurements be?

39-23-33. She would stand seven feet, two inches tall.

, •

What martial arts actor was so fast that they actually had to slow film down while shooting so you could see his moves?

Bruce Lee

, •

In November 2000, who was named an "Honorary Harlem Globetrotter"?

Pope John Paul II

How many people were murdered or imprisoned by the Nazis during the Holocaust?

15–20 million people

, .

The average iceberg weighs how much?

20,000,000 tons

, .

Who was the highest-ranking man of African descent ever in a European army?

French author Thomas-Alexandre Dumas (The Three Musketeers)

,.

How many ways can you make change for a dollar?

There are 293 ways

, .

What product is ten-times more effective at repelling mosquitoes than DEET, the main substance used in insect repellents?

Catnip

There are more of what animal than people in the world?

Chickens

, ·

What carnivore species has no brain?

Starfish

, ·

In 2007, what was stolen from someone's back yard without a single drop of water being found?

A 1000-gallon inflatable swimming pool

, ·

What two days out of 365 days of the year feature no American professional sports games (MLB, NBA, NHL, or NFL)?

The day before and the day after the MLB All-Star Break

, ·

What household cleaner was used to clean plutonium stains away in a defunct nuclear power-plant in Scotland as it was being dismantled?

Cillit Bang

What is the largest gland in the human body?

The liver

, ·

What are the two island Boroughs
of New York City?

Manhattan and Staten Island

, ·

What uncle was popularized by a famous
World War I recruiting poster?

Uncle Sam

, ·

Who was the self-appointed "high priest"
of LSD in the sixties?

Timothy Leary

, ·

What word originally meant a stew of many
different ingredients?

Hodgepodge

, ·

How many Academy Awards were won
were by "The Color Purple"?

Zero

Of the female elk, moose or reindeer, which one has antlers?

The reindeer

, •

What religious book is found in drawers along with the Gideon Bible in Marriott Hotel rooms?

Book of Mormon

, •

What instrument is used for measuring walked distances that works by responding to body motion?

Pedometer

, •

How many months do not have 31 days?

Five months

, •

Napoleon was known to have had ailurophobia, or the fear of what?

Cats

Like Peter Pan, what comic book hero has a brand of peanut butter?

Superman

, ·

What office building in Washington, D.C. was built in less than 16 months during World War II?

The Pentagon

, ·

What Clint Eastwood film was titled after a battle in the Korean War?

Heartbreak Ridge

, ·

What creature has been featured on the U.S. quarter in use since 1932?

Eagle

, ·

John Wayne has played over 120 characters during his career, but which one was Mongolian?

Genghis Khan (The Conqueror, 1956)

What company introduced the first commercially manufactured transistor radio in 1954?

Texas Instruments

, .

During his reign, who was identified by Fascists as "Il Duce"?

Benito Mussolini

, .

What 1935 introduction determines the magnitude of earthquakes?

Richter scale

, .

What board game features the Peppermint Forest and Gumdrop Mountain?

Candy Land

, .

What show created stars like Annette Funicello and much later helped launch Britney Spears, Christina Aguilera, & Justin Timberlake?

The Mickey Mouse Club

In 1998 Hilary Duff played Wendy the Good Little Witch, who meets what ghost?

Casper the Friendly Ghost

, ·

What satellite carried a dog named Laika into space in 1957?

Sputnik 2

, ·

What was the first comedy to be filmed before a live audience?

I Love Lucy

, ·

Who was chosen as Time Magazine's Man of the Year for 1938?

Adolf Hitler

, ·

What series of books had titles such as "The Poky Little Puppy" and "The Little Red Hen"?

Little Golden Book

What board game includes 2 blank wooden tiles and 100 with letters?

Scrabble

, •

The cables of San Francisco's Golden Gate Bridge were made by the same company that built what other famous bridge?

Brooklyn Bridge

, •

What actor said "Made it, Ma! Top of the world!"?

James Cagney (White Heat, 1949)

, •

What baseball team had winning records for 13 years in Milwaukee, but moved to Atlanta in 1965?

Braves

, •

What company trademarked the Frisbee?

Wham-O

The original title of what John Steinbeck novel was "Salinas Valley"?

East of Eden

, .

In 1959, what two states became the last two states to join the USA?

Alaska #49 and Hawaii #50

, .

The quote "It's alive! It's alive!" is from what film?

Frankenstein (1931)

, .

The "D" in D-Day actually only stood for Day and was simply used to preserve secrecy about what event?

The allied invasion of Normandy

, .

In 1953, the first of what Chevrolet sports cars rolled off the assembly line?

Corvette

What Yankees player had a 56 game hitting streak, and did not strike out during the 1951 season?

Joe DiMaggio

, .

What film featured the terrifying "Night on Bald Mountain" sequence?

Fantasia (1940)

, .

In 1937, what country began the emergency telephone number "999"?

Britain

, .

In 1947 Ed Lowe invented what absorbent product for pets?

Kitty litter

, .

Melted watches dot the landscape in what artist's "The Persistence of Memory"?

Salvador Dali

The boundary between what two countries was drawn with The Curzon Line in 1945?

Poland and Russia

, .

What was the cost of the first Playboy Magazine?

50 cents

, .

What Disney character debuted in 1934 and still wears no pants?

Donald Duck

, .

What character was voiced by Don Rickles in the "Toy Story" films?

Mr. Potato Head

, .

What was the typewriter correction fluid Liquid Paper originally called?

Mistake Out

Whose record as the youngest international grand master in chess stood from 1958-1991?

Bobby Fischer

, .

"Dawn of a New Day" was the slogan of what event?

1939 New York World's Fair

, .

What scientist was nicknamed "the father of the h-bomb"?

Nuclear physicist Edward Teller

, .

What old school game was included as an "Easter Egg" in the first Apple iPod?

Breakout

, .

In what country is it legal to marry a dead person?

France

, .

What animal can't stick out its tongue?

A crocodile

What was the Art Deco spire of the Empire State Building designed for?

It was originally designed to serve as a mooring mast for zeppelins.

, .

The owner of what electric vehicle company died on his own vehicle after driving it over a cliff?

Segway

, .

Italian physicist Alessandro Volta was made a count in 1801 for his invention of what?

The electric battery

, .

Charles Macintosh is best known as the inventor of what piece of clothing?

Raincoat (Mackintosh)

, .

What is the strongest muscle in your body?

Your tongue

How many times do you breathe in a year?

You breathe about 5 million times a year

, .

The average lead pencil will write how much?

It will write a line about 35 miles long or about 50,000 English words

, .

One fourth of the bones in your body are where?

In your feet

, .

The average person spends 2 weeks of their lifetime doing what?

Waiting for the light to change from red to green

, .

The world population is expected to rise to what by the year 2080?

15 Billion

, .

The largest recorded snowflake was how big?

15 inches wide and 8 inches thick

What moves so fast that the sound it makes is actually a tiny sonic boom?

The tip of a bullwhip

, ·

What is the Matami Tribe of West Africa's version of football?

Instead of a normal football they use a human skull

, ·

What soft drink would be green if the food colorant wasn't added?

Coca-Cola

, ·

During the 17th Century, who ordered his whole harem of women to be drowned and replaced with a new one?

The Sultan of Turkey

, ·

The handles on coffins used for cremation are usually made with what material?

Plastic

What is the longest word in the English language with all the letters in alphabetical order?

Almost

, •

How strong are human thigh bones?

Stronger than concrete

, •

A Ten Gallon Hat will hold how much water?

3/4 of a Gallon

, •

11% of the World is left or right handed

Left handed

, •

What is 111,111,111 × 111,111,111?

12,345,678,987,654,321

, •

How many quarter pounders can be made from a single cow?

400

A "Jiffy" is the scientific name for what?

1/100th of a second

, •

What aircraft's wingspan is longer than the Wright Brothers' first flight?

A Boeing 747 (Wingspan: 196' 0"-Wright Brothers first flight 120')

, •

A broken clock is right how often?

Two times a day

, •

A colony of 500 bats can eat how many insects?

Approximately 250,000 insects in an hour

, •

What is the only planet not named after a god?

Earth

If removed from the stress of the modern world, how much would you sleep?

The average human would sleep about 10 hours a day

, ·

Sneezing or burping is illegal during a church service in what city?

Omaha, Nebraska

, ·

What happened to the man who wrote "The Complete Book of Running"?

He died of a heart attack while running

, ·

Of all the words in the English language, what has the most definitions?

The word "set"

, ·

How many adults believe aliens are hiding on our planet disguised as humans?

One in five adults

What percentage of Americans eats breakfast every day?

38% eat breakfast

, .

How far do butterflies travel?

Scientists have tracked butterflies traveling over 3,000 miles

, .

The average American spends about a year and a half of his or her life doing what?

Watching commercials on television

, .

What is the only animal whose evidence is admissible in court?

Bloodhound

, .

How many insects can apple butter have before even the government says "Ewww!"?

The FDA permits up to 5 whole insects per 100 grams of apple butter

What is the longest recorded flight of a chicken?

13 seconds

, •

What creature consumes 86,000 times its own weight in 56 days?

A silkworm

, •

What is present in important meetings of the University of London?

The skeleton of Jeremy Bentham

, •

How many flowers would a bee need to pollinate to produce a single pound of honey?

A single bee would have to visit 2 million flowers

, •

In ancient Japan, who was required by law to be blind?

Traveling masseuses

What popular song features these words: "The chicken's in the bread pan picking out dough"?

Devil Went Down To Georgia (Charlie Daniels Band)

, .

It's impossible to become what if you're an atheist?

A freemason

, .

What popular building toy did Olympic gold medalist Alfred Carlton Gilbert invent?

Erector set

, .

Who flew on to the charts in 1987 with the instrumental titled "Songbird"?

Kenny G

, .

What type of cruise missile was first used by the U.S. Navy in Operation Desert Storm?

Tomahawk

Former professor, known as a domestic terrorist between 1978 and 1995, what was Ted Kaczynski's nickname?

The Unabomber

, .

Most bananas travel how far before being eaten?

4,000 miles

, .

What small dinosaur was named by Paleontologist Robert Bakker in 1990?

Drinker

, .

What state flag is called the "Crimson Cross of St. Andrew's"?

Alabama

, .

What bird has three stomachs?

Ostriches

, .

Who was pictured on the first postage stamp?

Queen Victoria

What black flag typically contains two femurs and a cranium?

Pirate flag

, .

In that classic freeway chase, O.J. Simpson was in a white Ford Bronco, if it had been a real live bronco, what animal would O.J. have been on?

Horse

, .

What animals got a bad name when there was a flu outbreak called H1N1 in 2009?

Swine

, .

What briefly replaced the leprechaun as the spokesperson for Lucky Charms breakfast cereal in 1975?

Waldo the Wizard

, .

What tops the list of most popular world languages?

Chinese

If you're allergic to eggs, which condiment would you skip at the sandwich shop?

Mayonnaise

, .

Giardiasis is an intestinal infection you can get from drinking water contaminated by rodents, also known as what?

Beaver fever

, .

The Baby Ruth candy bar was not named for the baseball player, but for what president's daughter?

Grover Cleveland

, .

Before and during the Civil War, who pushed to send freed black slaves to Central America?

Abraham Lincoln

, .

How many miles of blood vessels are inside every adult human?

100,000 miles

What percentage of all women in the U.S. have been married at least once by the age of 55?

Approximately 95%

' ·

Seattle's Space Needle was built for what event?

The 1962 World's Fair

' ·

In 1983 who became the first American woman & the youngest American to travel into space?

Sally Ride

' ·

What is the era of geological time in which we are now living?

Cenozoic era

' ·

What Olympic sport was Albert II, Prince of Monaco known for?

Bobsleigh

What is the world's best-selling rum brand?

Bacardi

, •

What agency of the U.S. government is concerned with providing clean drinking water to all Americans?

Environmental Protection Agency

, •

What color of smoke signifies the election of a new Pope?

White

, •

Josh Brolin's stepmom is what singer/actress?

Barbra Streisand

, •

The human body is made up of how many cells?

More than 35 trillion

, •

The U.S. Supreme Court ended what in public schools in 1954?

Segregation

The Ryder Cup matches are between pro golfers of what two countries?

U.S. & Great Britain

, .

Alex Cross is a police detective and forensic psychologist created by what author?

James Patterson

, .

Adam West, Ben Affleck, Christian Bale, George Clooney, Michael Keaton, and Val Kilmer have all portrayed what character?

Batman

, .

Who was the last English monarch ever to enter the House of Commons?

Charles I

, .

Who is the patron saint of lost causes?

St. Jude

What military medal is given to those wounded or killed in service to the United States?

Purple Heart

, •

What is the national and only official language of Andorra?

Catalan

, •

What is the science of heat and energy transfer?

Thermodynamics

, •

Who was the Patuxet guide who assisted the Pilgrims after their first winter?

Squanto

, •

What is a sailing ship with two or more masts called?

Schooner

What African-American military pilots flew in World War II?

Tuskegee Airmen

, •

Who was the captain of the Pequod in Herman Melville's 1851 novel "Moby-Dick"?

Captain Ahab

, •

Shakespeare's Hamlet was prince of what country?

Denmark

, •

How many bottles of Heinz Ketchup are sold around the world each year?

Over 650 million bottles

, •

Since overeating was a status symbol, early rulers of what state often weighed over 400 lbs?

Hawaii

Arkansas' Boston Mountains are the highest elevations in what mountain region?

Ozarks

, •

"With God All Things Are Possible" is the motto of what U.S. State?

Ohio

, •

Tom Cruise and Keith Urban have both been married to what actress?

Nicole Kidman

, •

90% of Americans over 15 have had what disease, also called Varicella?

Chicken Pox

, •

What state capital has been called "The Live Music Capital of the World"?

Austin, Texas

Who was the ruler of Rome
when Jesus was born?

Caesar Augustus

, •

What discharge is associated
with cumulonimbus clouds?

Thunder

, •

Who is also known as Lord Greystoke?

Tarzan

, •

What emperor legalized Christianity
throughout the Roman Empire in 313 A.D.?

Constantine

, •

In 2015, what MLB team won their
first title since 1985?

Kansas City Royals

, •

Who was the first female Speaker of the U.S.
House of Representatives?

Nancy Pelosi

At the 2001 MTV Music Awards, Alicia Keys pounded out what Beethoven song?

Fur Elise

' ·

A slave uprising against Rome was led by what gladiator in 73 B.C.?

Spartacus

' ·

What is the famous nickname of Manfred von Richthofen whose Fokker triplane was shot down on April 21, 1918?

Red Baron

' ·

What spirit is produced by distilling wine?

Brandy

' ·

On May 7, 1915 a German sub sank what British ocean liner?

Lusitania

In 2007, South Korean Ban Ki-moon took over what United Nation role?

Secretary-General

, .

What architect designed the Solomon R. Guggenheim Museum in New York City?

Frank Lloyd Wright

, .

God told Noah to build the ark 300 cubits long. How long is this in feet?

450 feet long

, .

Robert Griffin III was the first football player to win the Heisman Trophy for what Waco, Texas university?

Baylor

, .

Dry ice is made by cooling & compressing what gas?

Carbon dioxide

Who does the male subject in Grant Wood's painting "American Gothic" depict?

His dentist

, •

Katharine Lee Bates received $5 for the initial publication of what patriotic poem?

America the Beautiful

, •

What was the language spoken by Jesus and his disciples?

Aramaic

, •

John Wilkes Booth assassinated Abraham Lincoln in what Washington, D.C. theatre?

Ford's Theatre

, •

What amendment ended prohibition in the United States in 1933?

The 21st Amendment

Arranging colored pieces of marble, glass, tile, wood, or other material to form an image is called what?

Mosaic

, .

What Brahms composition would be used to rock your little one to sleep?

Lullaby

, .

What lively Central European dance is popular at weddings around the world?

Polka

, .

What is the machine that delivers a controlled electric shock to the heart?

Defibrillator

, .

What actress played Imperator Furiosa in "Mad Max: Fury Road"?

Charlize Theron

Andrew Lloyd Webber was best known for what musical?

Cats

, •

The Pacific Ocean was named by what Portuguese explorer?

Ferdinand Magellan

, •

Germany's "lightning war" attack on Poland in World War II was called what?

Blitzkrieg

, •

On Aug. 8, 1988, what Major League Baseball stadium got lights?

Wrigley Field

, •

What author was a KGB spy under the code name "Argo"?

Ernest Hemingway

Arthur Miller's only Pulitzer Prize came in 1949 for what play?

Death of a Salesman

, •

After the 1948 election, what newspaper ran the incorrect headline, "Dewey Defeats Truman"?

Chicago Tribune

, •

What is the only country in Central America that does not have a coastline on the Caribbean Sea?

El Salvador

, •

What world organization assists over 34 million refugees?

United Nations

, •

Marine iguanas are native where?

Galapagos Islands

Harvard, Princeton, Yale and Brown belong to what NCAA Division I athletic conference?

Ivy League

, ·

In March 2016, North Carolina legislators passed a bill that banned what?

Transgender people are banned from bathrooms and locker rooms that do not match the gender on their birth certificates

, ·

What German sausage is commonly boiled in beer, and served on a bun with sauerkraut?

Bratwurst

, ·

After having been crowned for a triumphant military conquest, who proclaimed "Veni, Vidi, Vici"?

Julius Caesar ("I came; I saw; I conquered")

, ·

Of the 12 zodiac signs, what one is named for the Greek god of war?

Aries

Known for his physical deformities, Joseph Merrick was the subject of what award winning play?

The Elephant Man by Bernard Pomerance

, .

What Jesuit Catholic university located in Cincinnati, Ohio calls their team "Musketeers"?

Xavier University

, .

What is the official birthstone for February?

Amethyst

, .

African American Crispus Attucks was killed in what 1770 incident?

Boston Massacre

, .

In 1938, Franklin Roosevelt founded the National Foundation for Infantile Paralysis, which was renamed what?

March of Dimes

Who wrote the "95 Theses", which stated two central beliefs—that the Bible is the central religious authority and that humans may reach salvation only by their faith and not by their deeds. ?

Martin Luther

, .

What award is given by the Columbia School of Journalism?

Pulitzer Prize

, .

What city was nicknamed "Rubber Capital of the World"?

Akron, Ohio

, .

Rikki Rockett was a hairdresser before forming what glam metal band in 1983?

Poison

, .

What is the nickname of Reno, Nevada?

The Biggest Little City in the World

The biggest single U.S. fundraising day for what organization is Halloween?

UNICEF (U.N. International Children's Emergency Fund)

, .

Who was the US Speaker of the House from 1995-98?

Newt Gingrich

, .

Your nose and ears never stop growing, but what is the same size since birth?

Your eyes

, .

The terrorist group ISIS took responsibility for three suicide bomb attacks in March 2016 that killed 32 people in what European city?

Brussels, Belgium

, .

Who received a Christmas Eve pardon in 2015 from California Governor Jerry Brown?

Actor Robert Downey Jr., for a 1996 drug conviction

What U.S. Document has been called a "bundle of compromises"?

The US Constitution

, •

The gospels refer to what as "the place of the skull"?

Golgotha

, •

Which designer became famous for selling men's underwear?

Calvin Klein

, •

What served as the boundary between Maryland & Pennsylvania, then later slavery and free states?

Mason-Dixon Line

, •

The American Lung Association was founded in 1904 to combat what infectious disease?

New York Daily News

What was the 2015 song recorded by Rihanna, Kanye West, and Paul McCartney?

FourFiveSeconds

, ·

Who was the 43rd U.S. President's wife?

Laura Bush (George W. Bush)

, ·

What artist was called "Painter of Light"?

Thomas Kinkade

, ·

Minnesota is called the land of 10,000 lakes, but what state has more lakes?

Wisconsin (nearly 15,000 lakes)

, ·

What city in Michigan was named after a war chief of the Ottawa people?

Pontiac

, ·

Who was known for these famous words: "Nothing is certain except for death and taxes."?

Benjamin Franklin

Who is the only elected official in the federal government with duties in both the executive & legislative branches?

Vice President

, •

How many books are in the Holy Bible?

66 (The Old Testament has 39 books and the New Testament has 27 books)

, •

What company supplied the American troops in World War I with double-edge safety razors as part of their standard field kits?

Gillette

, •

The modern knowledge on how the human body reacts to freezing is based almost exclusively on what?

Nazi human experimentation during World War II on Prisoners of Wars and Jews

, •

What is the only state whose postal abbreviation has a "Z" in it?

Arizona

What "Blurred Lines" singer is the son of "Growing Pains" star Alan?

Robin Thicke

What Native American tribe gave us the name for skunks?

Algonquian

On February 13 & 14, 1945 over 600,000 bombs destroyed what German city?

Dresden

Before 2012, who was the largest consumer of kale in the United States?

Pizza Hut — but only to decorate the salad bar

What is a detailed outline of a course of action for architects?

Blueprint

President Lyndon B. Johnson was known as an owner of what type of car?

Amphicar

, •

What two planets have no moons?

Mercury and Venus

, •

What is the practice of interpreting the influence of the stars & planets on earthly affairs?

Astrology

, •

What poet wrote "Where the Sidewalk Ends"?

Shel Silverstein

, •

An icon or animation to represent a participant used in Internet chat and games is referred to as what?

Avatar

What is the only one of the Seven Wonders of the World that still remains?

The Pyramids of Giza

, •

From the foundation to the top of the torch in the Statue of Liberty, there are how many steps?

There are 403 steps

, •

The Latin motto of the U.S. Marine Corps "Semper Fidelis" means what?

Always Faithful

, •

How can consuming a polar bear's liver kill you?

Because of its toxic levels of vitamin A

, •

What is the most recognized symbol of modern Jewish identity and Judaism?

Star of David

The Leptodactylus fallax, or giant ditch frog, is known as what on the island of Dominica?

Mountain chicken

, •

In 1211, Genghis Khan's force of over 50,000 soldiers broke through what?

Great Wall of China

, •

Women make up 70% of what country's lawyers and 60% of its judges?

Algeria

, •

What did Philadelphia native Guion S. Bluford, Jr. become in 1983?

In 1983, as a member of the crew of the Orbiter Challenger on the mission STS-8, he became the first African American in space

, •

What NFL team will relocate to Los Angeles for the 2016 season?

Rams

What is a Spiny Lumpsucker?

A type of marine fish most commonly found in the cold waters of the Arctic, North Atlantic, and North Pacific oceans

, •

In 1953, what Broadway musical's theme song became a U.S. State song?

Oklahoma!

, •

Former Vice President Dan Quayle appeared in an ad during the 1994 Super Bowl for what product?

Lay's Potato Chips

, •

21 different species of fish can be labeled and sold as what?

Sardines

, •

Meg Whitman became president & CEO of what computer giant in 2011?

HP (Hewlett-Packard)

What 1980 eruption was the first in the lower 48 states since 1921?

Mount St. Helens

, .

"Good Vibrations" in 1966 was what group's last Number 1 hit of the '60s?

The Beach Boys

, .

Who won 3 Super Bowls and owned a NASCAR racing team since 1992?

Joe Gibbs

, .

Big Ben in London lost about 5 minutes in August 1949 when a flock of what type of bird landed on its minute hand?

Starlings

, .

In 1955, 52-year-old Ray Kroc opened what burger joint, known for the golden arches?

McDonald's

Cass Ole was an Arabian horse, and the star of what 1979 film with Mickey Rooney?

The Black Stallion

, •

What NHL team earned their first-ever Stanley Cup victory in 1991?

Pittsburgh Penguins

, •

Who went from singing with the Funky Bunch, to Calvin Klein ads, and then on to starring in major motion pictures?

Mark Wahlberg

, •

What American rockabilly band was fronted by guitarist and vocalist Brian Setzer?

Stray Cats

, •

In Turkish, it's called "Hindi", In India, it's called "Peru", In Arabic, it is called "Greek chicken" in Greek it's called "French chicken" and in French it's called "Indian chicken". What native American bird is this?

Turkey

The animated character Max Headroom pitched what "new" soft drink in the 1980s?

New Coke

, ·

A giant turtle's intention was to destroy Tokyo in what 1965 film?

Gamera

, ·

Disney sent what actor a $1 Million Picasso painting as a way of thanking him for his work on "Aladdin"?

Robin Williams

, ·

When his coffin was opened in 1901, what former president's body and clothes were perfectly preserved?

Abraham Lincoln

, ·

In 1994, who was scheduled to perform a concert on pay-per-view, but took a $1.5 million loss due to the live TV coverage of the famous O.J. Simpson chase?

David Hasselhoff

Consuming even 15 milligrams of elemental Tellurium can cause your sweat and breath to smell like what for eight months?

Garlic

, •

The phrase "Always a bridesmaid, never a bride" was popularized by Listerine in ads featuring a lovelorn woman unable to find a husband due to what?

Her halitosis. The same ad coined the term "halitosis."

, •

17 countries will not accept passports for entry and 8 do not accept any passport with evidence of travel to what country?

Israel

, •

What character from South Park was inspired by Trey Parker's Father who told him that if he didn't flush the toilet, it would come out and eat him?

Mr. Hankey

What Marvel comic character is multilingual and omnisexual?

Deadpool

, ·

Thanks to specially designed grooves in the road, if you drive the speed limit of 45 mph for the quarter-mile stretch of what highway between Albuquerque and Tijeras can you hear "America the Beautiful" play through the vibrations in your car's wheels?

Route 66

, ·

What cats have such powerful jaws that they kill their prey by biting into the brain directly through the skull?

Jaguars

, ·

What statue was installed in Orlando, Florida where the homeless are banned from sleeping on benches?

A statue called 'Homeless Jesus', sleeping on a bench

Canada's longest running military operation involves what?

Firing artillery rounds at mountains to trigger small avalanches, which reduces the possibility of huge snow buildup and a bigger avalanche

, .

In 2014, a new species of vine was discovered in Chile that can do what?

It can mimic the leaves of many different host trees. It can change the size, shape, color, orientation, and even the vein patterns of its leaves to match the surrounding foliage.

, .

In 1450, what killed 40 people in Paris?

A pack of man-eating wolves led by a red wolf

, .

What did Nikola Tesla create and unveil at Madison Square Garden in New York City in 1898?

A wireless remote control

, .

As Secretary of State, Henry Kissinger delayed telling President Richard Nixon about the start of what event in 1973 to keep him from interfering?

Yom Kippur War

What is the longest-running running software product line for Microsoft?

Microsoft Flight Simulator predates Windows by three years

, .

Adidas will cancel any sponsorship deal they have with a player if it turns out he has anything to do with what?

Scientology

, .

What country has the best military record in Europe having won 132 of the 185 battles they fought in the last 800 years?

French

, .

Artist and engineer Julijonas Urbonasa designed a concept for what, which is designed to kill?

An art concept for a steel roller coaster designed to kill its passengers

, .

In 1985, Little Caesars created a kitchen on wheels called what?

The "Love Kitchen", which serves pizza to those in need and has responded to several disasters

Who was the highest paid athlete of all time?

An ancient Roman charioteer named Gaius Appuleius Diocles, who earned the equivalent of $15 billion before his retirement

, .

Although he was 6'5" and 315 lbs, whose mother would not let him play football in high school, afraid that he would get hurt?

Michael Clarke Duncan instead pursued his interest in acting.

, .

HBO, Showtime and FX all turned down what successful series?

Breaking Bad

, .

South Carolina Senator Strom Thurmond got married at the ages of 44 and 66, both times to who?

22-year-old winners of the Miss South Carolina beauty pageant

, .

What Japanese beef grade comes from pampered cows that are massaged with sake & fed lots of beer?

Kobe beef

Before her 7-day trip to space, what did NASA engineers ask astronaut Sally Ride?

They asked if 100 tampons was the right number for the mission

, •

In 2005, what did Swedish millionaire, Johan Eliasch purchase for the sole purpose of its preservation?

A 400,000-acre plot of land in the Amazon rainforest from a logging company

, •

Why did Tim Curry drop out of the 2002 "Scooby Doo" film?

He dropped out after learning that Scrappy Doo, a character he hated, was in the movie

, •

Who auctioned off his 1996 Olympic gold medal in March 2012 for charity?

Heavyweight boxer Wladimir Klitschko

Hans and Margret Rey were two Jews who fled Paris in 1940 on bicycles that Hans had built. They escaped just hours before the German soldiers seized Paris. Among the few possessions they carried was what?

An illustrated manuscript of the first Curious George book, which later went on to get published in New York.

, .

Rock singer Dave Navarro's mother was murdered in 1983. The murderer was her boyfriend who was arrested in 1991 thanks to a viewer tip after Navarro appeared on what television series?

America's Most Wanted

, .

Who said he didn't include online multiplayer support because of the small number of online players?

Sid Meier, creator of the original Civilization game

, .

What is the only Native American group that has never officially been conquered by the US government?

The Seminole Tribe of Florida

Who renounced his US citizenship in 2011 to avoid paying $700 million in taxes?

Facebook co-founder Eduardo Saverin, a native of Brazil

, •

Humans can live unprotected in space for how long?

About 30 seconds if we don't hold our breath

, •

The national animal of North Korea is what?

The Chollima, a mythical winged horse that they made up.

, •

What is the largest known star?

UY Scuti, which is 4,982,686,912 times bigger than the sun. It is only 9,500 light-years away

, •

What actor provided the voices of Snizard and Twin Man during the series "Mighty Morphin Power Rangers"?

Bryan Cranston, The Blue Ranger, Billy Cranston, is named after the star.

Ruth Lawrence, a child prodigy, passed what test at the age of 10, coming first out of 530 candidates?

The Oxford University math exam

, ·

The world's tallest skyscraper (not tower) is what country's Taipei 101, which stands 1,670 feet high?

Taiwan

, ·

From 1997 to 2000, Taco Bell used what as a mascot?

Gidget, nicknamed the "Taco Bell Chihuahua"

, ·

US Army during WWII developed what that was about the same size and shape as a regular baseball making it easy to use for the American soldiers who had grown up playing baseball?

The BEANO T-13 hand grenade

, ·

What baseball player was arrested in 1983 for killing a seagull during a game?

Yankees right fielder Dave Winfield

What is the oldest professional sports league that is still in existence?

MLB National League (1876). It predates the Football League of England (1888).

, •

Who missed almost five full baseball seasons while serving as a fighter pilot in WWII and the Korean War and still managed to hit 521 home runs?

Boston Red Sox slugger, Ted Williams (1918-2002)

, •

Who is required by rule to wear only black underwear, in case they split their pants?

MLB umpires

, •

Who was born a natural right handed hitter, but his father forced him to bat lefty saying he'd thank him for it later?

Prince Fielder

, •

Who is featured in the 'Roman beefcake calendar'?

It features a gallery of priests caught on camera during the Holy Week in Rome and Seville

What part of the internet was free until 1995?

Domain names

, ·

What movie monster's skin texture is inspired by the Keloid scars that grew on Hiroshima survivors?

Godzilla

, ·

What insects have the highest rate of STDs?

Ladybugs (Ladybirds)

, ·

Whose genome was so desirable that his sperm sold was for $25 million during his life and he has more than 200,000 daughters?

"Starbuck",a famous Canadian bull

, ·

There is a bill known as the "Cheeseburger Bill" which makes it illegal for people to sue food companies for what?

Making them obese (Personal Responsibility in Food Consumption Act)

An Oregon survey found that who were making more than the employees working inside Wal-Mart?

Panhandlers outside of Wal-Mart

, .

In 2007, the Malaysian space agency convened a conference of 150 Islamic scientists to determine what?

How a Muslim astronaut on the space station should pray facing Mecca

, .

In 1995, what magazine published an article scoffing the future of the internet?

Newsweek. The story is still available on their website.

, .

What restaurant has an 'angry burger' with hot sauce baked into the bun?

Burger King

, .

What is the fortune-telling board game known as the "Mystifying Oracle"?

Ouija

Diane Keaton debuted in the original 1968 run of what hippie musical?

Hair

, •

Who is still in prison for the murders his "family" committed in August of 1969?

Charles Manson

, •

Prior to their 1973 battle-of-sexes tennis match, Billie Jean King gave chauvinist Bobby Riggs what appropriate gift?

A pig

, •

What was Jim Morrison's reptilian nickname?

The Lizard King

, •

What two treaties were signed in 1972 & 1979 by the U.S. And USSR?

SALT agreements (Strategic Arms Limitation Talks)

What 1973 Martin Scorsese movie was set in Little Italy?

Mean Streets

, .

Who were first allowed to play Little League baseball in 1974?

Girls

, .

In 1975 what group informed us: "I wanna rock and roll all nite and party every day"?

KISS

, .

Who was the first gymnast to be awarded a perfect score of 10 in an Olympic gymnastics event?

Romanian gymnast Nadia Comaneci

, .

What future actor appeared in a 1982 advertisement for the Atari 2600 game "Pitfall"?

Jack Black

What was the first legal casino in the eastern United States, which opened in 1978?

Resorts International (Atlantic City, NJ)

, .

Ariane 1 was the first launch vehicle to be developed by who?

The European Space Agency

, .

In 1980, the Police released their third studio album, titled what?

Zenyatta Mondatta

, .

In early 1981, assassination attempts were made on what 2 men?

Ronald Reagan & John Paul II

, .

What was the line of portable pocket televisions introduced by Sony in 1982?

Watchman

What computer peripheral remained relatively obscure until the 1984 appearance of the Macintosh 128K?

Computer mouse

, .

"A Nightmare on Elm Street" introduced what actor on film before he jumped to "21 Jump Street" on TV?

Johnny Depp

, .

Oreos are actually a knock-off of what cookie brand?

Hydrox. They were created 4 years earlier.

, .

Lysol was originally marketed as what type of product?

A contraceptive

, .

What creature is mentioned in the KJV Bible?

Unicorns (Isaiah 34:7)

What movie was disqualified from receiving an Academy Award nomination for special effects, because the Academy felt using computers was "cheating"?

TRON (1982)

, •

George Lucas allowed members of what band to make a cameo appearance in "Star Wars Episode II: Attack of the Clones" in order to appease his daughters?

N'Sync (The footage was then cut out of the final version of the film)

, •

Apollo 17 astronaut Gene Cernan, the last man to walk on the Moon did what for his daughter that no other little girl would have?

He wrote her initials on the Moon

, •

What book was the result of a bet that its author could not complete a book using only 50 words?

Green Eggs and Ham (Dr. Seuss)

It's illegal for kids 16 and under in South Korea to do what past midnight?

Play video games

, •

Who presents the Trafalgar Square Christmas tree each year?

The people of Oslo, Norway, in gratitude to the people of London for their assistance during World War II.

, •

Who is the only player to hit a major league home run and score a touchdown in the NFL in the same week?

Deion Sanders, who is also the only man to play in both a Super Bowl and a World Series.

, •

What disease has killed half of all people who have ever lived?

Malaria

, •

What surprise did Burger King reveal on April Fool's Day 1998?

A "Left-Handed Whopper" specially designed for the 32 million left-handed Americans

What does the 94Fifty do, that a normal basketball does not?

The 94Fifty is equipped with sensors that measure spin and acceleration. With a mobile app, it helps you improve your shot

, .

Discovered in 2011, a bat was named after what "Star Wars" character?

'Yoda' Bat, native to Papua New Guinea

, .

Grown men ride a gigantic log down a steep hill to prove their bravery in what festival?

Onbashira (Nagano, Japan)

, .

In 1989, what did Geneva Steel do in an effort to show the company's importance to the local economy?

It paid its employees bonuses in $2 bills, which then started showing up in local businesses.

, .

How did Francisco Macías Nguema, former President of Equatorial Guinea celebrate the Christmas of 1975?

By having 150 of his opponents executed in a soccer stadium by soldiers dressed as Santa Claus

Who first cultivated lettuce?

Lettuce was first cultivated by the ancient Egyptians who turned it from a weed, whose seeds were used to produce oil, into a food plant grown for its succulent leaves.

, .

What did J.K. Rowling cite as the inspiration for how Harry Potter's Defense against The Dark Arts professor vacates their position yearly for various reasons?

The "This Is Spinal Tap" joke about the deaths of their drummers

, .

Cephalopods (Octopus) have been known to do what?

They can climb out of their aquarium, maneuver a distance of the lab floor, enter another aquarium to feed on the crabs, and then return to their own aquarium.

, .

What is the most common job in 29 out of 50 states in USA?

Truck driver

71 years before Rosa Parks, who refused to give up her seat on a train and was thrown off by a group of white men?

Ida B. Wells, She later cofounded the NAACP but was kept off the list of founders by W.E.B. Du Bois.

, ·

Roald Amundsen was a Norwegian Explorer, who in 1909 tried to become the first man to reach the North Pole, but was beaten by Robert Peary. Upon hearing of Peary's victory, Amundsen did what immediately?

He mounted an expedition to the South Pole, which he became the first person to reach in 1911.

, ·

After a large meal, what creature can sleep for up to 24 hours?

A male lion

, ·

A 1913, survey of U.S. children working under difficult conditions in factories found that 412 out of 500 would rather do what than the "monotony, humiliation, and cruelty" of school?

Work in sweatshops

What happened if the Nintendo game "Teenage Mutant Ninja Turtles III" was not an authentic copy?

The game silently reduces the damage the player deals out, doubles the damage they take, and makes Shredder immortal.

, ·

What country banned nearly all forms of motor-racing after the tragic 1955 Le Mans disaster?

Switzerland

, ·

What businessman did not consider his invention to be a major accomplishment and made no mention of it in his autobiography towards the end of his life, nor was it mentioned in his obituary?

Edmund McIlhenny, inventor of Tabasco sauce

, ·

What author served as a Lieutenant during World War I and fought in The Battle of the Somme?

J.R.R. Tolkien. It has been suggested that the horrors of trench warfare shaped his later depictions of Mordor in The Lord of the Rings.

Babies are born without what?

Kneecaps, which don't properly form until the child reaches 3-5 years of age.

, ·

Out of the 107 billion humans who have ever lived, how many have died before the age of 1?

An estimated 40%

, ·

After winning $17 million in the Florida lottery in 2006, Abraham Shakespeare went missing in 2009 and was found in 2010 where?

Buried under a concrete slab of an acquaintance's home

, ·

Who are widely credited with helping end segregation in Las Vegas, by refusing to perform in venues that wouldn't allow blacks?

Frank Sinatra and the Rat Pack

, ·

In June 2015, why was a man in Sweden was arrested for 'kidnapping' his own son?

Because his neighbors didn't recognize him with his new beard.

Thanks for reading!
If you could leave a little review on this book on Amazon.com that would be so helpful!
Don't forget to subscribe to my author central to get updates on my new books.

Go to my book on Amazon and click my name, then press "Follow" under my profile photo.

Thanks again
Bill O'Neill

Made in the USA
San Bernardino, CA
21 February 2017